Sport Bikes

By John Hamilton

VISIT US AT WWW.ABDOPUBLISHING.COM

Published by ABDO Publishing Company, PO Box 398166, Minneapolis, MN 55439.
Copyright ©2014 by Abdo Consulting Group, Inc. International copyrights reserved
in all countries. No part of this book may be reproduced in any form without written
permission from the publisher. A&D Xtreme™ is a trademark and logo of
ABDO Publishing Company.

Printed in the United States of America, North Mankato, Minnesota.
112013
012014

PRINTED ON RECYCLED PAPER

Editor: Sue Hamilton
Graphic Design: Sue Hamilton
Cover Design: John Hamilton
Cover Photo: Corbis
Interior Photos: All photos American Honda Motor Company except: Alamy-pgs 24 &
25; Getty Images-pgs 28-29; Kawasaki Motors Corp-pgs 2-3; Suzuki Motor of
America-pgs 11 & 12-13; Triumph Motorcycles-pgs 1, 8-9 & 26-27.

ABDO Booklinks
Web sites about motorcycles are featured on our Book Links pages. These links are
routinely monitored and updated to provide the most current information available.
Web site: www.abdopublishing.com

Library of Congress Control Number: 2013946168

Cataloging-in-Publication Data

Hamilton, John, 1959-
 Sport bikes / John Hamilton.
  p. cm. -- (Xtreme motorcycles)
Includes index.
ISBN 978-1-62403-222-6
1. Motorcycles--Juvenile literature.   I. Title.
629.227/5--dc23
                                                      2013946168

Contents

The Need For Speed

For some motorcyclists, there is no substitute for high performance. They want quick starts and stops. They lean into every tight curve. Every trip down the road is a fast thrill. Sport bikes were built for these demanding riders.

Honda
2011 CBR250R

What is a Sport Bike?

Sport bikes are built for excitement. They are the fastest, best-handling bikes on paved roads. They are lightweight and aerodynamic. Their powerful engines propel the fastest sport bikes to speeds of nearly 200 miles per hour (322 kph).

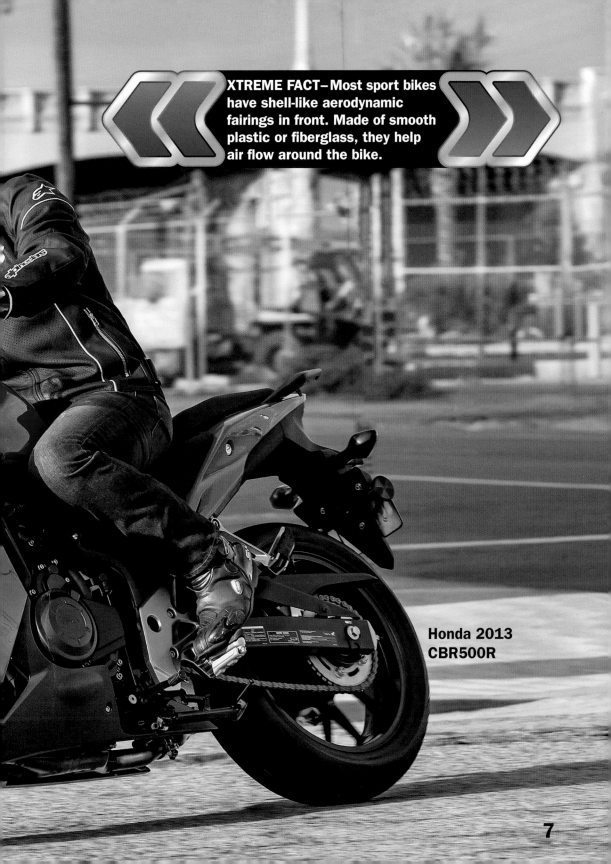

XTREME FACT—Most sport bikes have shell-like aerodynamic fairings in front. Made of smooth plastic or fiberglass, they help air flow around the bike.

Honda 2013
CBR500R

Parts of a Sport Bike

Seat Height: 32.3 inches (82 cm)

Triumph Daytona 675R

Lightweight aluminum frame

Compact exhaust silencer sits below engine

Rear Brakes: Single disc

Cast aluminum 5-spoke wheels

Wheel Base: 54.1 inches (137 cm)

LCD multi-function instrument pack, digital speedometer

Low-set handlebars for aerodynamic riding position

Fairing and screen protect rider

Front Suspension: Upside down fork

Front Brakes: Twin floating discs

Engine: 12-valve, 675 cc, 3-cylinder, fuel injection. Transmission: 6-speed

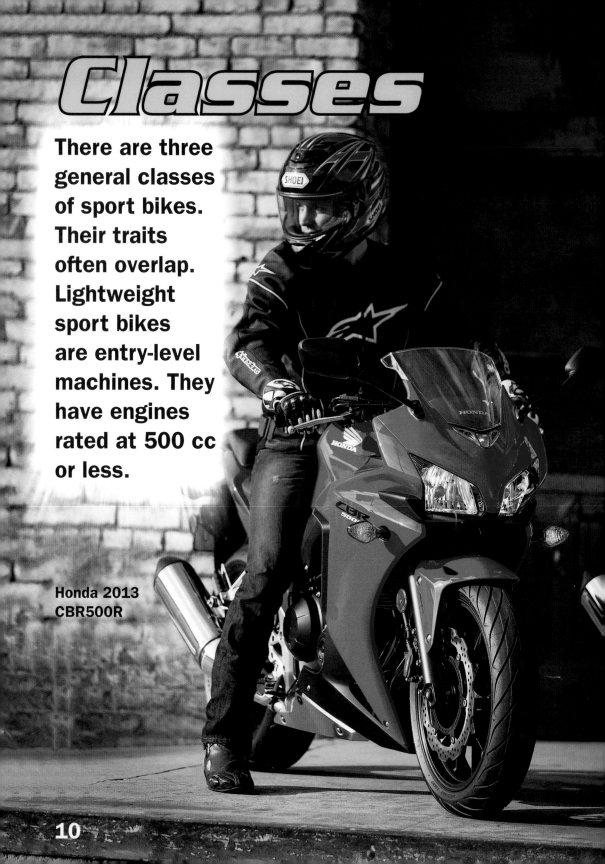

Classes

There are three general classes of sport bikes. Their traits often overlap. Lightweight sport bikes are entry-level machines. They have engines rated at 500 cc or less.

Honda 2013
CBR500R

Middleweight bikes, also called supersport, have engines up to about 750 cc. The most powerful sport bikes are called superbikes. They are road-hugging machines often used for racing.

Suzuki
2009 GSX-R750

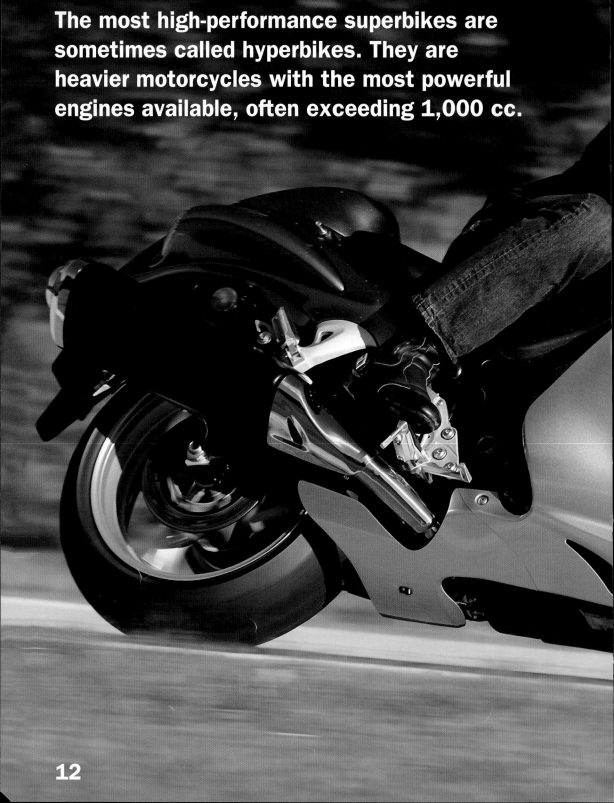

The most high-performance superbikes are sometimes called hyperbikes. They are heavier motorcycles with the most powerful engines available, often exceeding 1,000 cc.

2009 Suzuki Hayabusa
1340 cc

Engines

Sport bikes have powerful, two-, three-, or four-cylinder in-line engines. The cylinders are arranged in a straight line. The engines achieve very high RPMs (revolutions per minute). They give sport bikes incredible acceleration. Many sport bikes can go from zero to 60 miles per hour (97 kph) in under three heart-pounding seconds.

Honda 2004
CBR1000RR
Engine

**Honda 2004
CBR1000RR**

XTREME FACT–Engine power is partly defined by the volume of air/gas swept by the pistons inside the cylinders. It is measured in cubic centimeters (cc).

Rider Position

Sport bike riders reduce wind resistance by tucking their bodies down and forward. A raised seat and low handlebars reinforce this riding position. Riders lean their bodies into fast corners for added control. Sometimes their knees are only inches from the ground.

Honda 2011 CBR250R

Chassis

The frame of a motorcycle is called its chassis. Sport bike chassis are made of strong, lightweight metals such as aluminum and titanium.

2004 Honda
CBR1000RR frame.

Sport bikes weigh less than most other kinds of motorcycles, such as steel-framed cruisers. Most sport bikes weigh just 400 to 500 pounds (181-227 kg). Coupled with powerful engines, these light bikes can zoom down the road at very high speeds.

2004 Honda
CBR1000RR

Wheels and Tires

The rear wheel of most sport bikes is larger than the front wheel. The engine drives the big rear wheel. This extra road contact gives the bike quick acceleration and better cornering.

The front wheel of the 2013 Honda CBR600RR is slightly smaller than the rear wheel.

Under dry riding conditions, sport bikes used for racing have tires called slicks. These smooth tires grip the road for better handling. Sport bikes used for riding on streets have tire treads. They can be driven in both wet and dry conditions.

Honda 2004 CBR1000RR

Front Tire

Rear Tire

Brakes

Sport bikes not only accelerate quickly, they can also stop on a dime. During fast stops, much of a bike's weight is transferred to the front.

Honda 2012
CBR1000RR

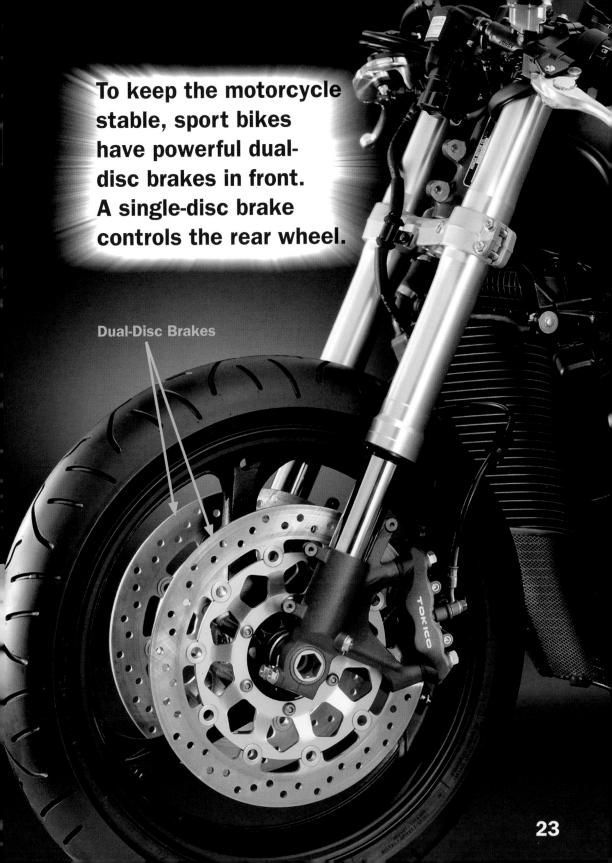

To keep the motorcycle stable, sport bikes have powerful dual-disc brakes in front. A single-disc brake controls the rear wheel.

Dual-Disc Brakes

Streetfighters

Streetfighters are sport bikes that have been customized in order to perform stunts. The fairing is often removed. Additions sometimes include large headlights and loud mufflers. High handlebars make it easier to perform stunts such as wheelies or stoppies.

A stunt rider performs a wheelie on a streetfighter bike.

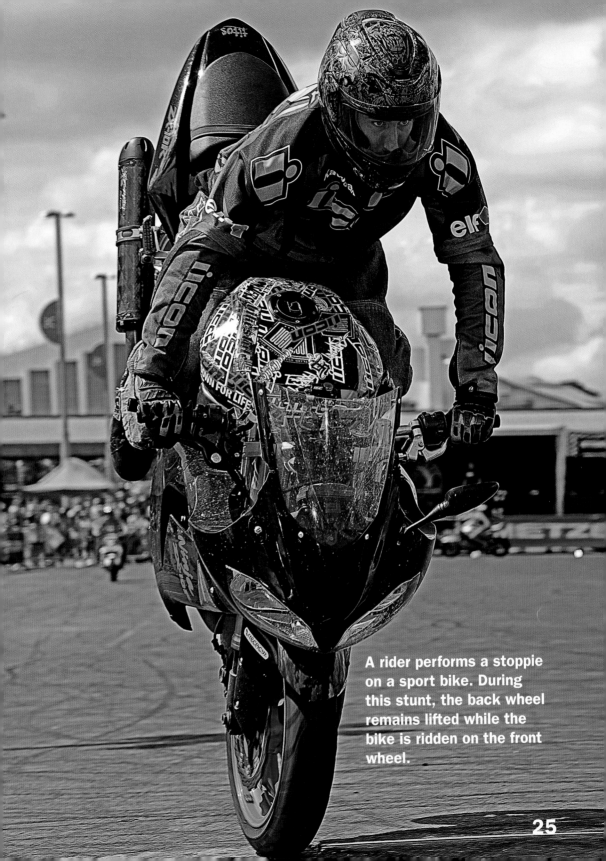

A rider performs a stoppie on a sport bike. During this stunt, the back wheel remains lifted while the bike is ridden on the front wheel.

Sport Touring

Sport touring motorcycles combine the thrills of sport bikes with the long-distance riding comfort of touring bikes. Sport touring bikes have large fairings and windscreens. The driving position is more relaxed and upright. They also have larger fuel tanks for longer cross-country trips, and built-in storage space for luggage.

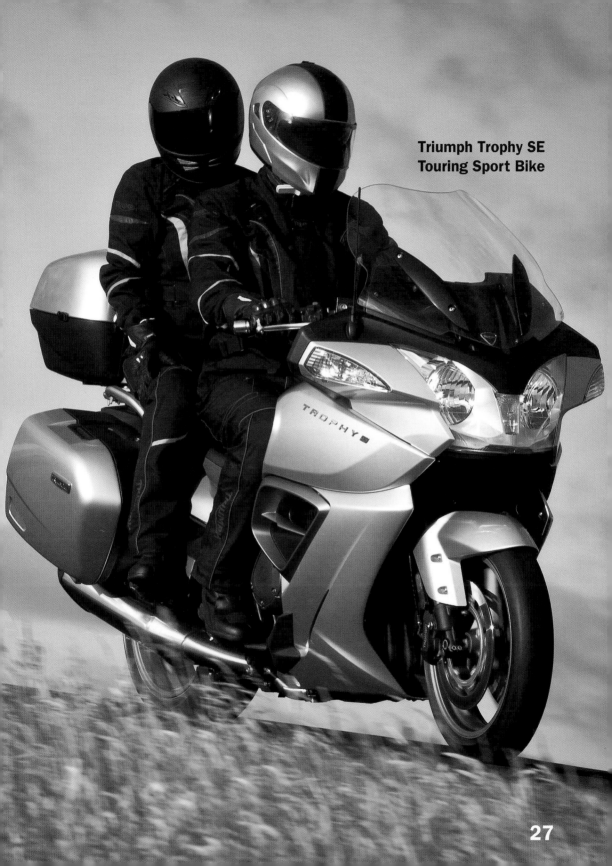

**Triumph Trophy SE
Touring Sport Bike**

Superbike Racing

Some of the fastest, most powerful sport bikes are raced on tracks worldwide. These superbikes reach speeds of nearly 200 miles per hour (322 kph).

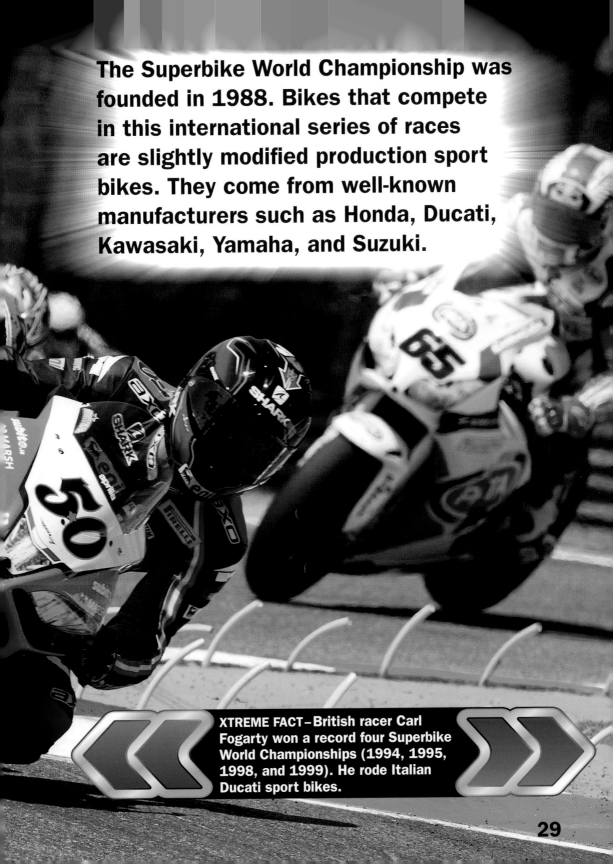

The Superbike World Championship was founded in 1988. Bikes that compete in this international series of races are slightly modified production sport bikes. They come from well-known manufacturers such as Honda, Ducati, Kawasaki, Yamaha, and Suzuki.

XTREME FACT–British racer Carl Fogarty won a record four Superbike World Championships (1994, 1995, 1998, and 1999). He rode Italian Ducati sport bikes.

Glossary

Aerodynamic

Something that has a shape that reduces the drag, or resistance, of air moving across its surface. Racing motorcycles that have aerodynamic shapes can go faster because they don't have to push as hard to get through the air.

CC (Cubic Centimeters)

Engines are often compared by measuring the amount of space (displacement) inside the cylinders where gas and air mix and are ignited to produce power. Displacement is measured in cubic centimeters.

Chassis

The body or frame of a vehicle.

Cruiser

A type of motorcycle where the rider sits in a laid-back posture with arms and feet forward. The Harley-Davidson company is known for its cruiser motorcycles.

Fairing

A plastic or fiberglass shell that is attached to the body of a motorcycle. Fairings help lower air drag and improve gas mileage. Fairings also provide a rider with protection against cold wind when driving at high speeds. In addition, the color and style of fairings give a unique look to a motorcycle.

Lean

How far a sport bike rider can lean horizontally to turn a corner as fast and efficiently as possible.

Index